FEEL EVERYTHING!
RUTH STACEY

Newton-le-Willows

Published in the United Kingdom in 2025
by The Knives Forks And Spoons Press,
51 Pipit Avenue,
Newton-le-Willows,
Merseyside,
WA12 9RG.

ISBN 978-1-916590-09-0

Copyright © Ruth Stacey 2025.

The right of Ruth Stacey to be identified as the author of this work has been asserted by them in accordance with the Copyrights, Designs and Patents Act of 1988. All rights reserved. No part of this publication may be reproduced, stored in a retrieval system, transmitted in any form or by any means, electronic, photocopying, recording or otherwise, without prior permission of the publisher.

This book is dedicated to the memory of
my kind and mischievous grandfather,
Jeffrey Oakey 1928-2023.

Contents

Introduction	9
Soft Leather Notebook	13
A School Teacher's Memo Book	33
Teal Green Velvet Covered Sketchbook	47
Cloth Bound Book with Gold Edging	67
Black Leather Notebook with PCS Embossed on the Cover	83
A Mottled Blue Business Ledger	109
A Small Brown Book to Fit in a Pocket	127
Notes	147

I

Introduction

Corinne Pamela Mary Colman Smith (1878-1951) kept seven different memoirs or journals in her lifetime, each one full of sketches, newspaper clippings and folded letters. They were all lost or destroyed. They are reproduced here for your pleasure.

Gertrude Käsebier, "Portrait PCS" The Critic, Volume 33, January 1899, p.15.

II

Soft Leather Notebook

Learn from everything, see everything, and above all feel everything! And make other people when they look at your drawing feel it too!

All you students who are just beginning your work in an Art School. Stop – think! First make sure in your own mind what end you wish to work for. Do you know? [...] As an exercise draw a composition of fear or sadness, or great sorrow, do not bother about details now, but in a few lines tell your story. Then show it to one of your friends, or family, or fellow students, and ask them if they can tell you what it is meant to portray. – **Pamela Colman Smith, Should the Art Student Think? The Craftsman, 1908.**

Realism is not Art. It is the essence that is necessary, to give a semblance of the real thing. – **Pamela Colman Smith, Appropriate Stage Decoration,** *Supplement to the New Age.* **June 2nd, 1910.**

I did not myself know I had any psychic powers – but others have said so. – **Pamela Colman Smith, letter to George Pollexfen, February 17th, 1902.**

Her gown and coat were long and floppy and of a sort of pussy-willow gray. On top of her curly coal black hair she wore a high-crowned gray hat, which in place of a brim, had a box pleating of bottle-green ribbon. – *Brooklyn Life*, **27th March 1909.**

At one time Alice Boughton, who, as was told in 'The Eagle' some months ago, has scored great triumphs in her photography, lived with her [...] Her (Smith's) metier was to lie in bed until midday, to do all her painting and designing under artificial light. – *Brooklyn Eagle*, **November 1st, 1904.**

An exotic young woman with melting dark eyes and a sweet, crooning voice. – *The Evening Statesman*, **Volume 36, Number 206, 27th February 1907.**

As there is no one word in English to express the idea contained in the phrase "dark-and-light," I have adopted the Japanese word 'no-tan' (dark, light). It seems fitting that we should borrow this art-term from a people who have revealed to us so much of this kind of beauty.' – *Composition: A series of exercises in art structure for the use of students and teachers* **Arthur Wesley Dow, 1899.**

A young designer, whose work has considerable interest, is Miss Pamela Coleman Smith. Miss Smith was a student of Pratt Institute, in Brooklyn, where her work, especially in coloring and decoration, attracted attention. She was a tireless worker and produced a great many posters, prints and designs, all peculiar for the wealth of decorative detail and the strength of the coloring. Among other labors of love, Miss Smith designed for her mimic theatre the entire scenery and costumes for eight plays, the text for which she wrote herself. This work showed a marvellous study of costume and great ingenuity and invention. – ***American Printer and Lithographer*, vol. 31, 1900.**

It is so hot here today I am sure Maud will not come.
– *Next day Tuesday 8.30am.*

Maud did not come.
But she may today!
– **Pamela Colman Smith, Letter to Mary B. Reed, 13th June 1898.**

More More More about Maud. She going to play Juliet! Law! and she and Russell are out at the races and things (have been seen) and if we can only get a hold of her we've got Russell! And he'll do anything to please her.
No sign of Maud Adams!
– **Pamela Colman Smith, Letter to Mary B. Reed, 10th August 1898.**

This pocket-sized book, covered in mauve leather, was brought by Pamela, nicknamed Melia by her mother, in 1893 when she visited New York aged fifteen to begin her studies at the Pratt Institute of Art under the tutorage of Arthur Wesley Dow. Even in his twilight years Dow would remember Pamela by her bird-like lilting laughter in class, which had disrupted the other students. The girl told many tales of her mismatched life. He could not get her to shush. Pamela used this notebook throughout her art studies, during which she met (soon to be more famous than her) photographers, artists, and writers. She wrote on the first page: *I will be successful.* Pamela visited the theatre many times to study a radiant human form wrapped in green fabric playing as Peter Pan and made sketches of her. The bookseller overcharged Pamela for the notebook, but she had a generous allowance from her father, who worked as an auditor for the West India Improvement Company. In 1896 Pamela returned to Jamaica to help nurse her sick mother, but she would continue to make entries into the notebook when she returned to her studies. Travelling back and forth between Kingston and Brooklyn, Pamela misplaced the book, leaving it on a shelf at a friend's house where it remained unnoticed. Despite Pamela scrawling, kindly return if lost and her address in the inside cover, it was eventually boxed up in a house move and sent to an eccentric second-hand bookstore. The owner, in irritation at it not being a saleable item, threw it into the corner of his storeroom, where it slept beneath the dust and detritus of decades, eventually falling apart.

Photograph by Alfred Stieglitz of PCS drawing. Unknown date. Reproduced with kind permission from Pamela Colman Smith: The Untold Story US Games Inc. (2018)

I will be successful.
Names are like butter,
they melt away
in the heat of new meetings.
Born beneath a full moon

in February. Carrying
water is a heavy
occupation for an artist,

it always runs through
my cupped hands.
        Grass grows on the cliff

edge, full of pink thrift,
look up to find I

        have nothing
                in my pockets.
Only a pencil, a wet ribbon,
a shadow to remind me.

No-tan – the paper is white, as we are lastly white.
Light reflects off bones uncovered from a barrow;
charcoal is being slowly burnt in the forest of firs.
The horizon, fort on a hill, the line of a profile
made interesting by the hook of a nose, the shadow
reflecting the cavernous socket of the closed eye.
Astronomical embroidery: join the dots to create
any shape you can imagine. Gods and fiends
jostle for space up there, their lines almost, but not
overlapping. Christ, I take your name in vain,
please believe me when I say it passes my lips
with nothing but tenderness in the out-breath.

Ambition is pale green
keep it in the
　　　　envelope of the mind.

Skill is a piece of flat quartz,
rubbed smooth.

Know the material of the ruff.
Hear the lute.
Go to the theatre, the ballet,

watch
how they express all feelings.

Remember your ~~poems~~ pictures
must not show clumsiness
no prettiness – rather you must
illustrate life.

Scarves hang over a headboard; stage set with a screen of colours. Feathers, beads, and hats scatter in the gaps. A camera is next to a pair of unlaced boots. Accordion folds of paper, brushes in pots and pencils worn to a stub. A plate of half-eaten asparagus drenched in butter. You *must* write to me using black lines on white paper. I will trace the shape of each letter with my fingertips. Think of me as you write so I can *feel* you as I read. There is a cat asleep between the spent young women. When one turns dust rises from the eiderdown and the cat stands, back arched like a bridge. Their two different perfumes combine to make a scent with a delicious, smudged label. Cat knows there is more languorous day-dream-sleep to be done, it waits for them to settle and curls up into a circle of warm, grey fur between them both.

Grumbles about light, about the ownership of light. This is the bulb I use to see. Plant it. Pushed into earth, light-coloured blooms bursting forth in spring. With a pull of the cord, they stumble and fall to their knees and cower in the darkness. Canvas and paper watch in aloof interest. The night wakens me. Electric guesswork of first strokes. Hung on a cord, this artichoke of filament and glass. My moon, always full.

Feel the *Prussian Blue* pushing
against the eyelids.
Oxide Green touches the arch
of an undressed foot.
Raw Umber brushes against
the neglected fold of an elbow
and leaves a *Red Ochre* rash.
Gold and *Silver* fill the throat.
Crimson and *Primrose Yellow*
burn foolish fingertips.
Approach with caution and use
only when vital to inflame the eyes.
Opening the paint box is personal –
the black lines contain the flesh.

The entrance hall is tiled with black and white squares. The Queen and the Actor wait beyond. Candles flutter and elongate the shadows into seven white birds with pink tinged wings. The darkness of the staircase is polished conker brown. The walls are patterned with lozenge shaped foliage, green and gold. Bowls of wild roses and apple blossom scent the air. Everything is ornate, decorative. Decorous satin shoes step silently. It is a stage-set for greatness. Have one aim: artist. What is inside my mind will appear on the outside. O! Beloved shapes!

Pan, stars are banished to be observers only. All they can do is wink, and nobody can decipher what they mean. It is a punishment. So, I am told. Maud. Moored. Then, untethered. Rope turns in the water like a yellow snake. Wooden boat catches the flurries. Forlorn lady lies supine. The Knight may mourn her, yet he does not notice that she longs for his battle-strong arms. The knight is a woman. Joan of Arc leads a white horse; it looks so sad. Her calves are shapely in the green tights. Gripping the balcony, leaning forward to see more. Joy as the leap across the stage takes flight: feather in the cap flutters. Skip, hop and elbows raised, and flute pressed against the lips. I took armfuls of painted scenery for you to view, but you were not there. I left my card. Never grow old. Wide sleeves decorated with leaves. I want endless curtain calls, so I can cast flowers at your feet. White-hot flames drop from the sky like rain. More, more, more!

Ice in the wind, slaps and snips, scissor cut.
Fragrance loops in flower petal curves,
the body floats in a garden at night.
Isabella holds her pot of basil.

I would keep your skull after death,
keep it close to me –
your bones are so well-made.

Sketches are studied on a dining room table. Viewed and discarded until the floor is littered with landscapes. The sad queen holds her hands together like an interlocked message. Silver crown is made of paper and foil. Where are her curled plaits? Escape from the castle, down the ladder made of copper wire – but she is not fully dressed Rising late, Maud's hair is not contained. Tendrils hang around her face, coiled snakes waiting to bite at any compliment. A white shuttlecock batted away. It is always summer here. Insects hum in the veins. Onlooker only – dismissive laughter is coloured mauve.

Asleep, I can hear the spider walking across the ceiling. The legs patter, louder than the percussion section of the orchestra. It is not the anecdote I wanted to begin with. Who is leading the spider? Does it wear a collar, a velvet girdle? If you keep a velvet ribbon in your pocket it is ready for any occasion: a garter to tie around a plump thigh or a noose to attach to the bar of the window. I can hear you thinking, what is the colour of the ribbon? Why does it always come back to colour? Ariadne's hair was black as soot scraped from the hearth. Elaine's skin was white as she lay back in her boat to die. Iseult's lips were naturally red, not tinted with rose petals. Olivia, dear one, beneath the terracotta sheet of our makeshift tent your veins stood out in blue lines. Ursula prowls the forest for honeycomb, growling her brown vowels.

Ruth Stacey

Pinned in place.
Stare and stare and stare.
Churned oil paint
depicts a ball of rock in the sky.
Silver grey. It makes a halo
of the eclipsed white sun.
Sunflower droops,
blend from black to pink.
It answers unasked questions.
It defeats and restores me.
I long to rip it from the wall,
take it home so I can
stare at it until my last day.

Gertrude Käsebier tells me her process. The how of it was explained: the dark room is a womb, the developing liquid amniotic fluid. The wait as the image appears is as lengthy as the time it takes to grow a foetus and birth it. An intake of breath, the long pause, then always, the delight at this new picture that didn't exist a second before. Revelation. Even if it is blurred, or the subject did not place themselves just so – the disappointment of the failed portrait follows the shudder of the nascent thrill.

Wrapped in tissue paper, lifting the translucent layer to stare at the vulnerable nape. Jet beads draw the eye down; lace shawl emphasises the delicacy of the flesh. Close-up. Filling the space of the image. Dark hair absorbed into the background. That one dominant eye captured clearly wanting. Jaguar with the skin of a sheep. Pose as a feeble muse but the gaze is an artist! Open to the viewer: my sins. Here is ambition! Here is determination! Here is yearning! Her camera removed my disguise. I burn my copy.

III

A School Teacher's Memo Book

I have a cover for a book of photos by Mrs Käsebier of Indians – she told RR she was going to get me to do it. Bobbie – the kitten has just walked all over this. **– Pamela Colman Smith, Letter to Mary B. Reed, 13th June 1898.**

Thank you so kindly for the horoscope [...] What you say of my mother and Father is quite true – I am sure my mother had ideas of her own –and was understood by very few [...] I think I was brought up in a rather unusual way – and there are plenty of people who do not understand me [...] I lived on and off in Jamaica about seven years – and heard a lot of folk stories – from the natives and two years ago published a book of them [...] Do you think I will be successful in my work? **– Pamela Colman Smith, letter to George Pollexfen, February 17th, 1902.**

Say Tutter, my daughter can't write for a cent but she can pen a sentiment [...] But at times the artist's assistant thinks she should have fresh water in her color pan and (he) flies to get it. He does not fly back, but saunters. Got it? Yes, indeed. **– Charles (Chas) Smith, postscript in a letter from PCS to Albert Bigelow Paine, 17th March 1901.**

Those who believe in inheriting of traits through parents will find ample confirmation in this girl. Her father was artistic to his fingertips, her mother one of the cleverest of Brooklyn's amateur drawing room actresses of her day. **– Winsome Witchery in London Drawing Rooms.** *The Brooklyn Daily Eagle*, **1904.**

'There could be no greater contrast to the ordinary, dainty heights girl, of pretty manners, or normal tendencies, conventional ways and the usual ambitions. Yet were an Iphetonga to be danced today, Pamela Coleman Smith, this odd-artist mystic girl, would be trebly qualified for its inmost place. *– Brooklyn Daily Eagle*, **1904.**

Of particular interest on this side of the river is this singularly gifted woman, for she is a niece of the late Mrs. Samuel Howard of Amity Street, and there are still many on the Heights who remember her mother, a brilliant young woman, especially clever in private theatricals which were often given at the Howards residence forty years ago. *– Brooklyn Life,* **1909.**

Pamela Smith and father are the funniest-looking people, the most primitive Americans possible, but I like them much [...] She looks exactly like a Japanese. [...] rather elderly, you are surprised to find out that she is very young, quite a girl. – **John Yeats, letter to his son William Butler Yeats, dated Monday, 1899.**

In the same line was her work with Irving and Terry for subjects. This latter attracted the attention of Miss Terry. The actress became interested in Miss Smith and when she left for England took with her the young designer. While I know nothing of the plans of either Miss Smith or Miss Terry, it is interesting to think that Miss Smith may be added to the staff of the Irving-Terry company as a sort of official designer [...]. – ***American Printer and Lithographer*, vol.31, 1900.**

'*Notes on Jamaica by Constance Smith*' was written by Pamela when she returned to Jamaica to help nurse her sick mother, until Corrine's death in 1896. The sick room always smelt of camphor. The curtains curling and yellowed from the sun. Corinne had ever been wily about her age. Blurring the years to lessen the decade gap between herself and her husband. Dear, foolish Charles, and dear, foolish Pamela. No mirror to the elegant Corinne herself, her child a foundling, an elf-child, or a cuckoo in a nest of larks. Always larking. They were giggling over some wax birds and missed the moment Mama breathed her last. Corrine died perplexed at them; puzzled is a very pale blue under closed eyelids. Pamela had jotted her memories of childhood in her memo book, remembering her Jamaican Nanny who taught her folk tales, thinking to turn them into something saleable. She wrote letters constantly, as if she were in a jail on the island and seeking release. She performed in writing the finest, most fun, most organised version of herself. She entertained children at the Half-way Tree Infant School Kindergarten and planned her art (and her secret hope to join the Lyceum theatre and spend more time with Ellen Terry). The book was lost in a house move and currently sits beneath a floorboard in Kingston. A mouse used part of it to line its nest; I cannot tell you the name of the mouse, as that is a secret known only to other mice.

Nanny said stories are pearls. Between the ages of seven and ten certain tales take hold in the body, grasp around the spine and ribs like oysters clinging to the rocks. These are the heart stories, the ones that keep it beating. You cannot undo them. People tell stories about gods, or stories about men defeating one-eyed giants and three-headed dogs, or women removing the heads of their enemy and serving them on a platter. They were not the ones that soaked into my skin. Black arms held me when we moved to the island. Cotton apron dried my tears. She was there in the early hours; her bed enveloped me when I didn't dare to wake my mother. And the talking bird says, *'An' you were so surprised at a dish of pearls; what would you t'ink if you was to know dat dese are sacred myst'ries.'*

Amusements –
all eager eyes turn
and expect something.
To entertain them scraps
are transformed.
Bring yourselves closer, children.
Paper theatres flutter.
Butter coloured fabric forms
a sandscape.
Tissue and thin sticks shape a stage.
It is a malleable age. Their eyes
see my goblins and fairies.
Miniature heart beats rustle –
snipped figures
crumple in my fist.

The heat of the day rises like escaping fowl. Soil slaking the heat from itself. Everything familiar and banal turns eerie in this new world of the garden. It is still mine, although I do not know it. Colour seeps, into sepia, into lavender, into grey. The paintbrush swirls in the water and is clean. Slip and blur. Moths flit and far-off an owl coughs out a pellet of bones. Let me begin: the beasts wear little coats and smoke pipes. The grass is wrapped around our feet. A fire is lit. Earlier, as the sun burnt out, bats swooped, and birds cackled. You say there are feathers in the yard where a beast caught our chickens. In this shadow space people cannot insert themselves, their features retreat, leaving pools of dark shading cross hatched, the flash of white from eyes and grin.

Dead mothers do not remind their daughters
to sit up straight. Corinne, it is always
night where you are:
this is what I think about as I fall asleep.
Below ground is one deep thought,
with the winding roots of the wheat
or the sinuous pomegranate plant.
In the mud, with simple, blind worms,
your slim arms, slimmer now.
Or in the sky, at the beginning and end
of all lives. It is a secret, and you are silent.
Sometimes there is brightness, Mother, from
the full moon and the white light, but it slips
into a half and then a crescent so sharp.
When the new moon is a negative disc
I worry about you, in the darkness, there.

Each train contains an ogre that pulls it along, the coughs and growls chug-chug-chug it through each station. Steam blanketing upwards and boiling metal squealing in pain. Windows are paintings that change. Galloping alongside the train, jumping each fence and wall, a little white deer rises to leap any barrier with a flick of his tail. Passengers stare into their newspapers and books, gossip quietly as the miles pass by. Mint sweets melt on the tongue. Pale feathers grow around the deer's hooves, joyful elevation onto clouds. Bouncing from one to another until it becomes a wooden deer in the palm again. Pocket-companion rubbed smooth for luck.

A Shakespearean alphabet for children,
a sure thing, a definite bestseller!
A is for Ariel, wisps of pale blue and green.
B is for Banquo, browns, ochres, sharp lines.
C is for Caliban, red slicked smudges. Grey?
D is for Dogbury, more reds and brown. Teal!
E is for Ellen, no, E is for Eleanor, Duchess
of Gloucester, royalty, elegant, and a witch!
Ellen, Ellen, Ellen. Write to me, invite me!
Pinks, yellows, flowers, flowers, flowers.
Travelling from place to place, learning lines.
Costumes: snipped cloth, sewn together.
Disguising, masking, embroidered shawls
and lace edged blouses. Long skirts, belts.
Packing, planning enough hats; which hats?
Black velvet one, the feathered one. Felt.
F for Ferdinand, G for Gertrude, H for Hamlet.
So gloomy. Grotesque. Impossible.
I is a complicated letter. Isabella too dispiriting.
Iago too frightening. Imogen's tale is not
for small minds. I can feel the rejection
letter, the crispness of the paper, I.

Grog. Why did someone call you that? Because you were a rum-coloured pony? Or sweet, like the drink? Did you knock people off their feet and give them a headache? Now you are dead, nothing but a spectre trotting around Jamaica, beneath the dogwood and palm trees. The pottery bowl is used to hold water, dip my brush. Crushed and unglazed, it bulks out clay. Little, sturdy horse, your name makes me giggle. My laugh is multi-coloured like a fool's motley. Hear the sound of it as the buggy dashes past *ha ha ho!* The notes rise like Grog's white mane caught in the hot breeze. Grog's biggest fear is harnessed oxen, he jumps with fright at the sight of the beasts. Nothing spooks me, not heights, or snakes or spiders. (I lie, I shiver like a horse at the thought of nothingness, of being no-one).

[Unsent Letter to a cousin]

Dearest! Please find enclosed a <u>fat, juicy letter</u>, rather ruined by cat's pawprints. A black and white cat; you would just <u>love</u> to see it! A kitty worthy of ancient Egyptians who would set about worshipping the little paws (even if they spilt the ink and smudged out half my words). I call him Cat. So, decipher what you can and be content with this scrap explaining the mishap. Painted birds come to life and fly at the window, so vexing. I continue here, looking forward to travelling to be with <u>dear Ellen</u> and company, real actors and stages instead of my paper imaginings! I am sketching and making and sewing, I just can't stop <u>doing</u>! All my love from Corrine no more, I am Pixie Pamela! (Do you like it? Ellen Terry gave it to me, the dear!)

IV

Teal Green Velvet Covered Sketchbook

Good acting appears so easy we overlook the fact that it is the result of fine technique. – **Pamela Colman Smith, Appropriate Stage Decoration,** *Supplement to the New Age.* **June 2nd, 1910.**

I know of no more delightful entertainment for children than yours, so quaint, so simple; and it is the prettiest of pictures, the children sitting agape around you. – **J. M Barrie.**

Miss Smith sat upon a low platform with her feet tucked under her, and a row of half-dozen big fat candles before her to serve as footlights [...] the young narrator presented a very picturesque figure gowned in a loose robe of flame coloured silk with an arrangement of tulle and beads bound about her head like a kerchief.' – **Pratt Art Club recital,** *The Sun NY,* **1907.**

She listened to many tales and legends of the unseen world, told by witchlike old women in the firelight, -- because in Jamaica no one dares speak of such things in the broad light of day, -- and she made a collection of them which she published as a book of Jamaican folk tales. – **M Irwin Macdonald, The Fairy Faith and Pictured Music of Pamela Colman Smith,** *The Craftsman,* **October 1912.**

"It is very interesting to see her," says one who knows, "dressed as 'Gelukiezanger' in parti-colored, gypsy-like gown and with beaded hair, sitting in Turkish fashion on the floor of a drawing-room, reciting her outland tales full of their queer conceits and unpronounceable names." She is an indefatigable worker, enthusiastic and rapid. – *The Reader: An Illustrated Monthly Magazine,* **1903.**

Pixie would entertain us and other children [...] Rather plump and very soft and lovable – we all adored her. – **Edward Craig, from 1975 interview with Melinda Boyd Parsons for the catalogue accompanying an exhibition of Smith's work at Delaware Art Museum, titled 'To All Believers.'**

She simply put on one of her gorgeous robes, wraps her hair in a queer oriental scarf, hangs a few strings of coral and amber beads around her neck and sits cross-legged on the floor with five candles twinkling before her. Her marvellous hands and her slanting eyes fascinate you, as she tells stories that old mammies in Jamaica tell [...] – **Gardner Teall ,** *Brush and Pencil,* **Vol 6, No 3, June 1900.**

The Japanese Toy. – **Ellen Terry,** *letter to Aubrey Campbell*, 4th **June 1900.**

"Miss Smith recited in the dialect, stories of folklore and fables of Jamaica where she lived for seven or eight years. She proclaimed a belief in fairies and goblins, which she said existed when her imagination could be set to work." – ***Brooklyn Daily Eagle*, 1909.**

This book was given as a gift to Pamela (Pixie), signed on the inside page *with much love from Gandy*. This was the nickname of the stately actress Ellen Terry, who had taken Pamela under her wing once her parents had died. Wing, sing, what kind of bird was Ellen Terry? Father and daughter had set off to live in England in the spring of 1899 to help Pamela set up as a professional artist. Sadly, in December 1899, the adoring, cheerful and accommodating father (who had returned to Brooklyn on business) died. Charles Smith, gone, aged only fifty-three. Pamela drew three portraits of him from memory, with the third being agreed by all to be very like him. The green book detailed Pamela's adventures with the Lyceum Theatre tours and her work as a hustling storyteller and illustrator. She excitedly details her meetings with the Yeats family, with much glee and an ever-present irreverence. <u>Underlining</u> and exclamation marks!!! Green ink. Deep loops on the hanging letters and slanted text. She practised her artist signature all over the inside covers. There are countless (76) pictures of her friends in the margins, including Henry Irving as a stork and Bram Stoker as a large bat. Despite it being a beloved possession of Pamela's, her last companion, Nora Lake, threw it into the fireplace after Pamela's death in 1951, due to what Nora felt was taboo content. It was bothersome to burn and took many turns in the embers to fully dispose of it.

Cocks a crowin', green fields explodin,' and the sly sun
butter-fat in the azure expanse beyond. Blue shroud.
How, with primroses underfoot, is there a telegram?
Black type saying: He will not see you again, child!
All eventful things seem to happen on a Friday –
because the goddess forgot about the mistletoe,
my nose, my eyes, my cheeks, my mould – gone.
Voyaging without his compass, no one to hoot at his
jokes – each one a mouse that can no longer scamper.
Curled up in a wheat stem nest, O! Let him sleep then.
I am a laughing girl on a white pony,
my father running out of breath to catch me.

Gandy, I called you, and you petted me. In your orbit
I was Io, I was Calisto, I was Europa. One of many.

In a forest of elms, you were the birch that the birds
chose to make love upon. In a room, all turned to you.

Leading me, you opened the curtain and showed me
the stage, with all the costumes and props.

Shakespeare, the Russian Ballet, everything huge
and glittering and poetic. Nothing prosaic.

If one could design a mother, not the half-remembered
thing, but a magnificent body, with a lilting voice

and the scent of jasmine at dusk,
that is the mother I would paint and with a spell

bring to life so that my voice is answered by hers.
Pixie, she would say, come out and play with me.

And I would answer, yes, I will be your devil:
I will caper, entertain, amuse you, be your jester.

The ship crossing the ocean is a theatre; the parts are acted without words. The turn of a foot, the swoop of a cape. Henry Irving is so devoted to his chosen art that even the drinking of his morning coffee from a tin cup, watched by a seagull on the deck, would bring an audience to their feet to cheer.

Encore!

Uncle Brammy and Gandy approach like metals balls drawn to a magnet. A piano is played, and her best dress is worn. Notes circle the ceiling, and the portholes are full of teal-green waves. Sea creatures swim near to the ship to listen. Two magpies sit on the branch of an elm tree. They teach me.

Two little Devils, Pixie and Puck:
Hecate calls us to make mischief.
Hear the quire of magical folks,
their singing is full of mirth.
This feels unholy, but so sweet.
The charm of magic tempts –
pale blue prayer is far away.
The ship cuts through the waves
and the salt settles on warm skin.
Merry wanderers, all else asleep.
We hear a screech owl, a frightful
noise so far from land: we run
and hide beneath a canvas cover.
Den of small creatures who cling
for warmth; idle slumber talk.
Pixie, you whisper, *do you lead
travellers astray? Are you partial
to a saucer of milk?* Pixies
do not age; live in foxgloves,
collect shiny things and trick.
Puck, you are the leader of all
the fair folk, the songs say so.
You direct all events. I act in crowd
scenes and paint the scenery
with a horsehair stick.

The naming of Pamela Colman Smith. Wardrobe full of coats. Silk, cotton, wool. Shrug one on, one off. It crumples at the feet like a bear skin. Where is the skinned animal? She has fled at the sound of a woman calling her name: Mela. One kiss and the skin fell off to reveal the golden body beneath, royalty after all. All unnatural wilderness banished. If the animal body hadn't shuddered in fear and galloped away, what might have happened in that moment? Constance, Con: a trick that I play on you. Little red-headed devil. Unpinned, it was dark auburn at my nape, in the light, copper. Polished by ancient Britons into a torque. Placed around a lover's neck. Remove one letter. D. Am I evil? I can gambol, I can entertain, I can be charming, I can clean your kitchen if you leave out milk. Pixie. Honey, all sweetness, invented by a poet. Pamela, are you listening? Be as Picky as you like. Prickle me. Tiny, silver bells sewn into the folds of the jacket announce mystery. Ting, ting, ting, ting. Choose a different coat, Miss Smith.

A mildewed man who looks
like a haughty owl is speaking.
The mind is bordered
by little hedges
filled with folklore's
creatures. The yew hedges
transform into water –
flow from one
person to another.
Between us a singular
energy and vision shared.
The owl twits and they all twooooo.

Storytelling for hire: *In a long-before-time – before Queen Victoria came to reign over we* – flame coloured robe glows with embers, green hooded scarf hides my face. One slim hand gesticulates as I sit cross-legged on the floor. My stories flow into portraits. Gather closer. Are you listening, dear ones? Creating the prettiest of pictures, children sitting around, mouths agape. Why, even Mark Twain became a boy in my presence. His laugh had misplaced punctuation all through it. Telling stories, you need universal, world-old ways. It is a spell of course: a charm. Stir the mixture under a new moon. Bury it in the garden with the heart of a shrew. Brew it with rose hips and dandelion stems. I am not serious. Beguiling. Holding everyone spellbound. One thin green snake.

Lily, white flower embroidered onto a grey field with a greyer moon hanging above. Three stems of steel coloured barley and lengthening teal blue shadows. Instead of paint, silk. Such quiet work, the circle of sewers. Needle sharp pricks, the tiny silver thimbles chime like bells when hit by accident, prevent the red blood staining the scenery. The bull has wings like an angel – cream, gold, pink, fuchsia, purple feathers surround him as he clutches his bible.

A cloak is shaken between them, forced together – drink a potion to wipe the memory of it.

Lolly, a hill rises like a loaf and, above, the sky takes up too much room. Pale wisps curl and wash into the washed-out blues. The foreground is a path leading one into this heavenly expanse. It is saying, up here there are no responsibilities or duties or guilt. Printed papers fly like gulls, all with double quotation marks.

Lady of the Lyceum.
Night-child, wood wanderer.
Dress sewn with green beetles,
queen of all the rooms.
Misty-kind shape-shifter,
eye-absorber, theatre-filler,
captivating she-colour
invigorating the scenery.
Play acting being young,
quite nicely, and oddly.
Hater of fogs. Immortal beast.
Long white throat lifting
the marvellous head as lines
are recited –
and illness, causing
the throat to contract into
dryness and silence. As if
the blood has been sucked
from the veins, leaving
an ache for wellness,
a throb for the slick-red
voice to return.

Reveries, the wall is green. A door leads to our past lives, so we keep it locked; I peep through when everyone else is in bed. So beautiful! Such fun! It is a land of hills and rivers. Lilac scented cream on my skin. A woman is on stage. Her bodice is trimmed with ermine and her skirts are embroidered with red tulips. On her wrist, a hooded falcon. How it pulls to get away! The woman loves her spirited falcon, she strokes it tenderly. The jesses are fitted with silver bells. They chime and I wake. Edy floats through the hallways; her nightgown is sky-blue cotton. I kneel to see how her magic works. Edy, I say, what are you reaching for here? Her fingers make the shape of a bull. My hair is curled into buns held in place by flowers that were grown for the wives of sultans. Edy issues an edict.

Visit to Bruges. Chris and Edy, Gandy and I, all adventuring to visit a sculptor. Room over a baker's shop with four beds and four chairs. A tiny window with no curtain which must be covered as the queen hates light in the night. We cannot breathe. The carillon chimes causing confusion each hour. Blasts of trumpets follow our procession through town. A king is nearby. Sing in my crooning voice. There is a thing we cannot mention at dinner, and it keeps coming into our mouths like a rat trying to scurry out of a hole. Picnic in a pine forest, brown smell of rotting tree debris. We can see our way. Here is the sculpture and the sitter, a woman, made from clay. Nearby, the head of her dead husband is taking shape from a sketch. The curls in his hair have tiny cupids hidden in the folds.

Lamp and firelight fill the corners.
Gandy in her throne-chair smiles at us
as we tell stories.

Edy impersonates all visitors,
guising in and out of characters.
You are always *you*, she laughs.

Smiling, nodding, grinning –
Pixie agrees with her, but I
burn.

Words unravel like a dropped ball of wool.
Not one thread,
       enough
to string all the lutes I imagine.

Photograph by Alice Boughton from the Brooklyn Life January 1907

Gelukiezanger – my stage name. The audience whisper when they hear my borrowed stories. The reviewers write childlike. Naïve. Simple. Perfect for children. Charming, they say. I transform it like a spell. A gypsy woman stirs the celebratory drinks, a native girl dances across the floor, a Jamaican folk tale teller speaks. My Pilgrim ancestors chide me for my mischief from their graves. A family tree can always have new branches. Perhaps I am a foundling? Wrapped in leaves and exposed under a juniper tree? My games only exaggerate their sweetly gifted judgements. I am Father's female double. My Brooklyn Heights pedigree is not high enough: Yankees make English folk sneer subconsciously. I laugh at them and draw myself in different guises; wrap myself in a kimono. I magpie everything into a costume of confusion.

V

Cloth Bound Book With Gold Edging

You ask me how these pictures evolved. They are not pictures of the music theme – pictures of the flying notes – not conscious illustrations of the name given to the piece of music, but just what I see when I hear music –thoughts loosened and set free by the spell of sound. [...] for a long time the land I saw when hearing Beethoven was unpeopled, hills, plains, ruined towers, churches by the sea. After a time I saw far off a company of spearmen ride away across the plain. But not the clanging sea is strong with the salt of the lashing spray and full of elemental life; the riders of the waves, the Queen of Tides, who caries in her hand the pearl-like moon, and bubbles gleaming on the inky wave. – **Pamela Colman Smith, Pictures in Music, The Strand Magazine, 1907.**

Pamela Colman Smith has seen through many veils. To her the universe is a congeries of suggestions. She has smitten with the rod of her imagination this adamant world of such seeming solids and vaporised it. And out of this vapor she has shaped her visions of life, her symbols done in color, her music matrixed and moulded to concrete shape. – **Benjamin De Casseres, Camera Work, July 1909. No. 27, pp. 18-20.**

The drawings are strong and full of the mystic, impressive power. Miss Smith's conception of the 'Appassionata Sontata' is a swanlike figure, huge and having the face of a woman, billows and turrets, or they may suggest trees to some observers. – **The Brooklyn Daily Eagle, Monday, March 18th, 1912.**

If Miss Smith is affected by music and produces work of such a distinctive delicacy, charm, subtlety, why that is her own psychology. Certainly, some of the Debussy illustrations are as satisfactory as their tonal originals. Debussy thinks so himself, owns and admires an entire portfolio. – **The Sun (New York) Sunday, March 17th, 1912.**

The door was flung open, and we saw a little round woman, scarcely more than a girl, standing in the threshold. She looked as if she had been the same age all her life and would be so to the end. She was dressed in an orange-coloured coat, with black tassels sewn all over the orange silk, like the frills on a red Indian's trousers. She welcomed us with a little shriek. It was the oddest, most uncanny little shriek, half laugh, half exclamation. It made me very shy. It was obviously an affectation, and yet seemed just the right manner of welcome from the strange little creature, "god-daughter of a witch and sister to a fairy" who uttered it. She was very dark, and not thin, and when she smiled, with a smile that was peculiarly infectious, her twinkling gypsy eyes seemed to vanish altogether. Just now at the door they were the eyes of a joyous, excited child meeting the guests of a birthday party. – **Arthur Ransome, A Chelsea Evening, Bohemia in London, 1907.**

One day a young woman appeared [...] she asked me to look at her work [...] since it illustrated exactly what I was feeling at the time and what was in danger of happening to the Photo- Secession I decided then and there to present her work. – **Alfred Stieglitz.**

This book is housed in an archive of someone's belongings and correspondence, but it has no identifying name on it, so it is catalogued as, 'Item 416: journal with entries describing paintings/ or perhaps dreams. Author unknown.' The true story of the journal's origin can now be told. One afternoon in London, Pixie-Pamela hurried into a small, dusty shop to get out of the rain. There were books piled up on every surface and the bookseller was an elderly man with an accent she could not place. Consonants tumbled from somewhere up North. He offered her his chair by the fireplace to get warm, and after accepting a hot drink, Pixie felt obliged to purchase something. The books were so dusty she did not feel like browsing through them, so she asked him to pick her out a book for a reasonable price. He crinkled his eyes most charmingly when he smiled (she thought he was smiling but she could not see though his luxuriant grey beard) and shuffled off into a back room. Returning, he put a book in her hand and said (at least that is what she heard) *no charge, Mystic*. Pixie did not look at the title but bowed and said a sincere *thank you* and dashed off to meet her friends at the Lyceum theatre. Later, remembering the book, she pulled it out to look at it. The title said, *Visions*, but the pages were blank. She filled it with all the following entries that detailed her daydreams of music and ghosts she encountered.

Chris and Edy allow me to live with them. A tripod has three painful points. Four floors, five ghosts. The drawing room was rented by a woman keen on hauntings, table rapping and spiritual meetings. She left because the ghosts used such bad language. Old English words for the body. Stale incense is always wafting in the air from the Catholics who lived here long ago. No one could live or work in the haunted room, but I move in. Cat, in a sandy coat, curls up on the bed and purrs. I hear footsteps, thuds in the night. If I look out of the diamond shaped window, I can see a monk digging beneath the old fig tree, trunk older than the house, in the dappled grey garden. The spade catches the silver sparks of starlight.

No one believes me when I tell them that birds are transparent; the sunlight burns through their disguises. Feathers and bones pretend life. Cats know. They hook them from the air. Claws extend to pull the flitting, sweeps of emptiness down to the earth. They leave them uneaten because they are nothing. Rats, mice, shrews, despite tasting of detritus and foraging, get eaten. Often only a head, or the bottom half cleanly disappeared, sometimes the guts arranged on the doorstep. Cats have rituals that are beyond our understanding. Birds are eerie, they have eyes without feelings. Cat has feelings – boredom, contempt, pity, disgust, greed. On the morning of the important decision, Cat plucked a most generous present from the air. A perfect robin on the doormat. Blood sacrifice, an offering, pagan magic. Shuddering at the thought of bad luck, and the pity of the pretty redness, fear consumed me. Cat knew better. The sacrifice to the old gods, of hawthorn and corn and fire and flowers and blood, worked.

The tundra rolls on in my dreams. Steam rises from velvet muzzles; something howls far off in the glacial air. Float across continents to see it. Stare down with a dispassionate eye. White fur, jaws red with blood. The feathers clog the mouth and the beast snaps in impatience. O! My familiar fox! Illuminate the sky with the discarded bones, grind each one into fragments and cough them into the waiting blackness to become the stars. Now we are beneath the pine trees. Make haste! Searching through my grimoire for a spell that will work, turn me back into a woman. O! Desperate hare! O! Carpet of resin-smelling needles!

The curtain rose bloomed.
Scheherazade talks her life
into another morning.
Bird-bodies beating their wings
into flight; the docile soul lifts
away from the blacksmith
thrashing on his anvil.
Kingdom of dusk-dreams,
evoking a half-remembered
expression of agility.
The chariot seeks beauty!
Core of the mosaic,
single frenzied tile – a veil
of blood lifts to reveal love.
Mortals move whilst dancers
express the immaterial soul.

In front of my vision, a hole in the air. A shutter snapped shut. It is an inch square. I see a wooded bank and broken ground. One bay horse blends in with the tree trunks. Smooth-skinned young trees; leaves fluttering to an invisible breeze. I cut a piece of paper to echo what I saw. Little elfin people, their clothes billowing. Skirts and sleeves let bluish light through; limbs dance to the orchestra I hear. Paintbrush in my fingers, curled in a corner: I listen and paint. Quick, quick! It must happen fast. Do not hesitate or think! Just let the paint define stripe, shadow and movement. The music etches lines. Swiftly waft the notes into colour, as soon as flutes and piano stop, the image fades into nothingness. Hark!

Schumann's *Carnaval*
plays on the gramophone.
The wine glass fills and empties.
Supine on the chaise, pencil
dropped to the floor,
a gaze remains in the mind.
A royal blue cat-woman stares
with a half-smirk – recently slaked.

Two sweet lovers are also adrift.
They cling together in the woods,
but they will find their way to her
cavern –casting a glamour,
she will invite them in,
and O! Poor custard fools!

They will enter her teal-green
foliage, they will drink her grape-
juice, they will slumber forever.
The Sphinx will smile –
her cat tale twitches back
and forth as she purrs,
one paw resting on all the bodies.

The Craftsman October 1912.

Claude Debussy wants to tell me something. He smiles; I paint his music and his dreams are now visible. Musical notes as paint. Symphonic sketches. The last note is Db. The people who dwell there enter the scene; they wander idly from group to group. Stifle my thoughts. The air is in the lowest octave. A stately queen, wearing brown, sings about bells ringing in the sky. My arms are held by whirling cords connected to hers, joined as long as her voice holds the notes. At a gathering in a salon, someone murmurs behind their fingers. I lean closer to hear the half-spoken whispers. I sway to the harpist in the corner. My skirts are velvet, my necklace is made out of lapis lazuli. Chinwag. His wife shot herself in the stomach with a revolver, and the bullet lived in her flesh; she still breathes. I too have a bullet in my body. I am on the top of a mountain. There is a freshness in the air. The dawn is opal coloured.

All the mer-folk are female. Maidens. My lady. Roe falls like rain through the water. It is clear and sticky. My translucent veils whip in the wind and create echoes of clouds. To make Opal Hush pour claret into a glass and add lemonade from a siphon until you get an amethyst foam. Stars fall to earth to hear the sea-maid's music, so someone said. Far-off an embroidery delicate ship out of reach. Tips of the sails show what could be. It is going, going. I sit cross-legged as if on a magic carpet, unconcerned by the tumult below. Cat, in his black, silken body, lies on my feet. Sea horses appear in the air. Faces, mouths, bodies, entwine in water. So many shades of purple, violet, lavender and mauve. I could reach down and touch, but I hold my voile up to catch the northerly wind and progress.

Beethoven's Opus 84 settles in the canvas of the mind. Pensive brushes of purple reveal a mountainous landscape. This is no rolling hillside, but impassable sharp peaks. Wash the purple to reveal the effect of perspective, to show how far away sunrise is seeping the heavens with light. Here, though, the mountain is shaded. At her foot worshipers hold staffs and raise their soft, human arms in awe. She ignores them. One strong arm curves to cup her chin with her hand. The weight of her head is rock itself. Is she heart-sad? Or bored at their attempts to converse. Grape blends to navy, the slightest soaking of teal. Above, the mountain cliff is a headdress, diadem of ancient days. Goddess of the mountain. Three, thin trees lift their bare branches as if trying to flee. A mage stands there with his yew staff and amethyst robe; two women wait to be sacrificed. One is sat quietly, sadly, in a one-shouldered toga. The other, naked, lies flat on the mountain rock, close to the edge. Her chin held in both hands, as she absorbs the wonder of it all. The mountain goddess below, cares not.

Idle women appear in robes that hang.
The paper is filled with long sleeves,
gowns that sweep, swishing cloaks,
faces that show ordinary emotions.
Fear, disgust, melancholy, longing.
Curve of the ink turns the domestic
into clouds, foliage, trees, towers.

Breathe in the page-fragrance.
Geraniums, green, bruised in passing,
honey-yellow sweetness, tang of yew.
Cat, on the oak table behind me, hisses
my real name but no one hears him.

VI

Black Leather Notebook With
PCS Embossed On The Cover

Dear Mr Stieglitz – I wonder where you are!! I want some money for Christmas! [...] I've just finished a big job for very little cash! A set of designs for a pack of Tarot cards I shall send some over –of the original drawings as some people *may* like them! – I will send you a pack (finished in colour by a lithographer) – (probably very badly!) as soon as they are ready – by Dec 1 – I think. – **Pamela Colman Smith letter to Alfred Stieglitz, November 19th, 1909.**

Two people over here want to buy copies of Peter Pan Photograph – & I told them they would be five dollars a print but they want them! [...] Do please tell me frankly if you think the work is better or worse! It is a great help –criticism! – **Pamela Colman Smith, letter to Alfred Stieglitz, January 1st, 1908.**

Pamela Colman Smith is so naturally a mystic that she has but little intellectual interest in mysticism. From childhood she has had the gift of second sight [...] On the continent, her friends were Maeterlinck, Debussy, and others who were endeavouring, each in their own way, to pierce the veil that hid the subjective world. Pamela Colman Smith had not the great creative power of these men, but it soon became evident that she had something as rare – the power to see clearly the invisible realm of which they all dreamed. – **M Irwin Macdonald, The Fairy Faith and Pictured Music of Pamela Colman Smith,** *The Craftsman***, October 1912.**

I have embraced an opportunity which has been somewhat of the unexpected kind and have interested a very skilful and original artist in the proposal to design a set, Miss Pamela Coleman [sic] Smith in addition to her obvious gifts, has some knowledge of Tarot values; she has lent a sympathetic ear to my proposal to rectify the symbolism by reference to channels of knowledge, which are not in the open day. – **The Occult Review (Volume 10, Number 12),** *The Tarot: A Wheel of Fortune***, Arthur Edward Waite, 1909.**

Now in those days there was a most imaginative and abnormally psychic artist named Pamela Coleman [sic] Smith, who had drifted into the Golden Dawn and found its ceremonies - as transformed by myself - without pretending or indeed attempting to understand their sub-surface consequence. It seemed to some of us in the circle that there was a draughtswoman among us who, under proper guidance, could produce a tarot with an appeal to the world of art [...] – **Arthur Edward Waite,** *Shadows of Life and Thought***, 1938.**

Pixie Smith alone seems to understand what I want. – **W.B Yeats, letter to Lady Gregory, 1904.**

Wouldn't you know it, just to look at her? We were talking about Edmund Dulac's illustrations of fairy tales one day and she said indignantly: "But his *goblins*! Why, he doesn't know anything about goblins! Goblins don't look like that!" You see, she *knows*.
– *Delineator*, **November 1912.**

'Le loup criait sous les feuilles
En crachant les belles plumes
De son repas de volailles :
Comme lui je me consume.'
– *Une Saison en Enfer*, **Arthur Rimbaud, 1873.**

Alongside her visitor's book (which does survive) Pamela kept a journal about her time in the Hermetic Order of the Golden Dawn, intending to write a memoir from it one day. She gave it to 'mildewed' W.B Yeats (also described by her as a rummy critter who over-performed for the ladies, but a good teller of folk tales once the distraction of attractive women was removed) who she knew was interested in the spiritualist and visionary details, but he leant it to his fierce lover Maud Gonne. Maud was reading it in a carriage one day, when she got distracted by a commotion in the street. Exiting the carriage, the lady forgot the memoir and it was left on the cushions and found by the driver. Making head nor tail of it he gave it to his wife who used it to prop up their guest bed – it had always been crooked causing guests to complain of a stiff neck. After years of this abuse, it crumbled and was swept up and thrown into the dustbin.

The Craftsman - The Craftsman, Vol. XXIII, Number 1 October 1912.

In the Isis Urania Temple
secrecy is rose-pink and silver,
it glimmers on the edge of
ordinary things and makes
them extraordinary.
Both sexes practice together.
The dawn is golden, the tree
of life has three orders.
Divine utterances and rituals:
the green ivy plant tangles.
Initiation then progression,
through each unfolding door.
Staging, spectacle and us,
the willing audience.
This is a kind of theatre for
the practice of mysticism.
Each needs a motto:
to yourself as to others.
A reminder to stop acting
parts and be my secret self.

Red forking-tongue and slink-length,
coiling around a limb.
Be afraid of the drought-breath, fill
the iron bath to the brim.

Skin delightful hauntings glow,
sucking black honeycomb.
Feasting on a pretty doe;
blood soaking through the loam.

Cloven-hoofed steps patter-hop –
witches settle on branches.
Flame births an attercop.
O! Spells are avalanches!

The sun rises in the east turning the city from grey to gold. Elixir of luck is passed around at a meeting, fragranced oil lifted from a blue wooden box decorated with sunflowers. Orange, fresh smelling. Even Yeats surreptitiously rubs it on his scrawny neck. A speckled bird sits on his shoulder. Florence Farr whispers to me. Meditating in the British Museum surrounded by Egyptian artefacts, eyes half-closed to daydream the priestess into life. She is covered with red and green striped cloth, holding a lotus wand. She is lame when she walks in my dream – her hip was hurt when she was a child striding by the Nile. She wears a thick golden anklet in the shape of a snake to equal out the misfortune. A jewelled girdle circles the whiteness of her cotton waist. The cards are read and reveal nothing. Rough images, drawn by someone who does not feel. A new deck is proposed.

Schism. Hands held in ritual prayer, one left and one right, palm full of magical energy, the other holy power. I lean towards the sea. A cupped seashell is used as a lamp. Filled with an oil pressed from gold, it burns incessantly. Steps lead down into the earth. Mushrooms with yellow undersides are poisonous. Two hundred and twenty steps down. A chamber, a man. He breaks the lamp so people cannot learn its magic.

Waite snuffles with a cold as he directs me in what I already know. The tarot deck we are using as a guide has clear symbolism for the major arcana. Still, he must tell me things. Chastise me, so I bite my lip, nod. He is knowledgeable but a dull colour. He is beige-grey. Or yellow, like the lichen you get on trees. When others are there he speaks as if I am not! A selkie. From woman to seal, flapping in the corner, longing for the sea-salt escape. Hear him, saying I am a visionary but need guidance, that only he can bestow. O! I long to tip the candle onto his pompous cloak and burn him – not to death! Just to char him a little. Warm his chilly single-minded ideas into something that catches an ember. No doubt, I will catch his cold, but I suffer on; there is a little money in it.

Wands are a lance, no! A wooden stave.
Cups are a grail, no! A simple goblet.
Swords are swords are swords.
Pentacles are dishes. No! Money, coins.

    Fire, water, air, earth.

Flame, sea, clouds, mud.

    Ember, salt, mist, compost.

Coal, eddy, fog, clay.

    Purpose, emotions, intellect, money.

Dream it, feel it, face it, make it.

All the joy is in the chalice, all the fear is in the mind, all the success is in the coin, <u>all contentment</u> is in my purpose.

> Note: *these ones are mine, all my imagination, all my friends, all my experiences, all my hopes, all my dreams, all my horrors.*

Ruth Stacey

Le loup criait sous les feuilles
En crachant les belles plumes
De son repas de volailles :
Comme lui je me consume.

Loup; loop; look closer. Attention to detail. Meaning transcribed from a single word. You see, Reynard has too much personality. No foxes here. Vermin. Vixen. Wolf and chicken at odds. Forest wild and farm contained. Fox and chickens, more comfortable. A domestic villain. Isn't the farm dog woken by the noise? Lifting his head and smelling the musk of fox; hearing the squawk of death; sensing the joyful gluttony. Wolf and dog. Two halves of one identity. Primal and tame. Id and ego. What more could be said about a blackbird with all white feathers? The card is clear in its symbolism; the moon is the secret side of the self. Moon. Moot. Moat. The moon is a warrior returning to battle each night, never learning that it will be defeated. *Dear Mr Stieglitz, did you get the money for the moon?*

Loup — loop – circle.

O

<u>It clearly says wolf</u>. Translators write/transcribe wolf. ~~Loup~~

well-thumbed   pocketed   held
    over-read   prized copy

said: fox
whispered: fox
alleged: fox
cried: fox

The fox cries in the bush
spitting out the bright feathers
from his feast of fowl
like him, I consume myself.

Perhaps it is a not a circle, but a circular room with a door, the poet inside and the translator locking it. The key is made of solidified ink and is washed away in the rain. Run! Try to soak up the flood with your embroidered (a pattern of crayfish stitched with teal-blue French knots) handkerchief.

Describe it dispassionately. The moon is full and hangs like the interior of a skull. Below are two beasts, one wild and one domestic. The dog howls; is she spitting out the feathers from her feast of fowl? Moon pulls the tides, back and forth. Inside the body, such a large percentage of water, pulled by the moon? Tidal flesh. The waves of effect upon the psyche. Lunatic. Hysterical. Daylight is a mink, white in winter, wrapped around my neck with its teeth held to my artery. Poised to sink in, sharp as cactus spines. I am stranded barefoot on the rocks. No moonlight either, no starlight, the moat is full of water and the bridge is lifted. Knights cannot enter with their spears. The room is drawn with walls and a door; an electric light bulb to light the canvas.

Loup, not Reynard, but the translated poem said *fox spits out the bright feathers of his feast of fowl*. Feather plucking, stripping, lightness, air, flying, eiderdowns, sleeping, dreaming. Spits out the feast. Feast: to gorge or celebrate. Richness, excess, gluttony, saliva, mouth, tongue, lips – to spit angrily? Joyfully? Softness of feathers on the lips. Do wolves or foxes have lips? And are the feathers flying upwards, so they float down, caught on a morning/evening breeze; and do the feathers catch on nearby bush cover like sepia decorations? The golden hour or darker, more cover, no clouds or thick downs of wetness suspended above the ground and the moon halved, waxing or waning – whole like a plate? O! disc of butter! O! paint palette! O! circle!

C'est le Diable qui tient les fils qui nous remuent!
Aux objets répugnants nous trouvons des appas;
Chaque jour vers l'Enfer nous descendons d'un pas,
Sans horreur, à travers des ténèbres qui puent.

Ainsi qu'un débauché pauvre qui baise et mange
Le sein martyrisé d'une antique catin,
Nous volons au passage un plaisir clandestin
Que nous pressons bien fort comme une vieille orange.

The Devil pulls the threads that move us!
Things we should not want are full of charm.
Every day we descend closer to hell,
feeling no horror, though the darkness reeks.

Like a weak sensualist who touches and licks
the decorated breasts of an ageless Jezebel,
we steal along this secret path,
squeezing the dried orange for one more drop.

There is a wooden signpost, and it tells of two different ways to go. One decision and your life will change. Is it this then, this uncertainty: which way now? There are horses grazing in the distance and hills that could go anywhere. A white tower looms. I have always loved a landscape with a horse in it. The black horse snickers with joy. Yet people are my preference: cheekbones, limbs, flesh, costume. That is what I am drawn to. Drawing. The horse is the gallop across grass, unburdened. Paint four stallions, courtly men on their backs – their shying from a scare: off stage. Their rearing, frisking, bucking: hidden. Falling to the floor: unseen.

All drapery discarded –
nothing but grass below and sun
boiling clouds into wisps above.
No wind trembles the green cupped leaves
on the white birch that crowd the bank.

Slant over the silver river,
unbound brown hair breaks the surface.
Water lilies observe this.
Strands become sodden as water
climbs the hanging ropes to land.

Stairs built in gold bend under the weight of all the splendid women in Greek dress. Burne-Jones paints them into *his* woman: angels with the same melancholy, fearful face. Their fingers and toes tremble through the canvas; afraid to take step and clinging together. A dancer cannot be a masquer, blue cannot be green, and fields of stubble are waiting to be burnt. A cloak dyed with the rarest colour ground from an impossible insect. A headdress made with quills too heavy to wear. Mock-dance the gestures and steps. Chanting beautifully and a golden voice are not enough ingredients for magic to occur. Worshiping serpents results in scales falling from the lips. Violet, silver, green. The chiffon dress is covered in sequins to resemble a snake, each sinuous movement shimmers.

the moon watches on, crescent cupped to
hold the fire filled sky, how it laps
excited demons released from the labyrinth
an arrow points to where they should be
it is a knot that is impossible to unravel
I am pulled apart, tendons, heart valves
skin dissembles into poplar fluff

twirls and curls, the oil seed rape is
heavy in the air, yolk yellow fields

      the minotaur is here but not here
the wind the wind
absorbs all the howling of the little foxes
they crawl up and down, arms raised
it cannot be undone

the knot is a house sized tear drop
decorated with water-flowers
all the foxes must walk the threads
that form the shape of this

one beautiful white fox wears ballet shoes
she drifts through the air
the moon is crying and grinning
all but one of the foxes' arms are raised
O! it is unfathomable!
      the shadow of the bull
is in the arched doorway of the maze
bring oil, a stick, linen, a flame

In my dream again, a great church
on a verdant hill, surrounded by a garden
hedged with trimmed box arches.

Rooks and magpies calling overhead,
but it is not frightening.
I move towards the place and arrive
there without any time passing.
The statues that flank a tomb are cut
in sandstone, festooned with green moss.
Out of the corner of my eye their feet
and fingers move slightly.

Music floating. A procession arrives.
Solemn notes sound as mild-faced,
pale spirts waft past me.

Each one cradles a blood-red heart
suspended from it, a pearl.
They slip past me to pass away
into the long, blue door of the church.

Over the rim of the cup, I see bronze feathers. An angel is waiting for a steak cooked bloody in the middle. I will cook it when I have poured my drink. The meat waits on the table, bleeding on the plate. An angel's hum is just out of human hearing – an insatiable pause between lightning and strike. Grating the spice, and stirring, takes aeons. He sighs. In the armchair, the magnificent legs fidget, cramped wings tremble. *There is no heartbeat.* I smile; he will wait whatever the discomfort. One feather falls onto the rug, its curved barbs submissive, asking to be stroked. The spiced milk is warm, and I pour. The angel reaches over and turns over the cup, no liquid falls. He smirks, a parlour trick. Dove-light, it slips down the throat. After this, nothing will sate.

VII

A Mottled Blue Business Ledger

Feel Everything!

Dear Mr W.B – I am writing to tell you a plan that Mrs Fortescue and I have in our heads – which you might be ale to think over on your trip home – we want very much to set up a hand press – to print small editions of books (by subscription) [...] in either case will you do the text for us? – **Pamela Colman Smith, Letter to William Butler Yeats, February 3rd, 1904.**

The publishers and public are just as bad here won't buy anything – & if they do don't pay!!! – **Pamela Colman Smith, letter to Alfred Stieglitz, February 21st, 1908.**

Between you and me and the wall, as they say, Miss Pamela Smith (though I think her a fine illustrator with a fine eye for colour and just the artist for illuminating verse) is a little bit lazy, and she being a woman I can't take a very high hand with things, so there is often a lot of fuss about the numbers, and I don't like to be responsible for anything that I have not got absolute control of.' – **Jack Yeats, letter to John Quinn, 15th December 1902.**

Pixie is starting another paper – an affected, dilettante sort of affair, but as her Irish god 'Mr Willie' has blessed it, she thinks it will be the most original journal ever produced. – **Ellen Terry letter to Christopher St John.**

I used to go to her studio once a month and colour Jack's pictures while she did hers, only a hundred. Yet she often lay on the sofa and cried because, she said, I was bullying her and making her work when she did not feel like work. – **Lily Yeats, to Ruth, 15th November 1937.**

The noticeably weak point in Miss Smith's work is the lettering. – **American Printer and Lithographer, vol. 31, 1900.**

Her gift meant nothing. If they had understood her meaning; if they had known their parts; if the pearls had been real and the funds illimitable – it would have been a better gift. Now it had gone to join the others. – **Between the Acts, Virginia Woolf, 1941.**

There was a swish of dresses, a stir of chairs. The audience seated themselves, hastily, guiltily. Miss La Trobe's eye was on them. – **Between the Acts, Virginia Woolf, 1941.**

Ruth Stacey

ALONE, and in the midst of men,
Alone 'mid hills and valleys fair;
Alone upon a ship at sea;
Alone – alone, and everywhere.
– **Pamela Colman Smith, The Green Sheaf, no.4, 1903.**

This business ledger, filled with notes on sales, plans for new work and pages of plain paper pasted in and filled with memoir about Pamela's time producing art for sale. Using turquoise ink, and as usual many exclamations and underlining, Pamela describes her escapades trying to earn a living in the world. She co-edited, with Jack Yeats, a publication titled *A Broad Sheet* in 1902. In January 1903 she created her own journal, to enable her to have control and avoid the pitying looks she got from the Yeats family. Pamela called it: *A Green Sheaf.* Storytelling, hand-colouring illustrations, publishing, and her moment of triumph: an exhibition of her work in New York at Alfred Stieglitz's gallery in 1907. She soon realised, after much later correspondence, he was seeking a different artist to promote (Pamela would later peer at Georgia O'Keeffe reproductions in their small-vastness and sense it was to do with welcoming nature and open feminine sensuality, something Pamela tried to avoid). In fact, during this period Pamela had locked all her desire for oranges up and converted to the Catholic faith. She would spend the rest of her life giving all her unrequited passion to the Virgin Mary. Or perhaps not. Pamela buried this ledger in the back garden of her London home, inside a box containing a portrait Jack Yeats had made of her sitting between his sisters Lolly and Lily. Jack had drawn her holding a yellow frog and Pamela, usually brashly forthright, had never dared to ask why.

PCS, 'self-portrait' Chim-Chim: Folk Stories from Jamaica, The Green Sheaf Press, 1905.

Apply here, prophetess, woman-child,
scarcely more than a girl.
Wrapped in feathers and silken scarves.

Audition for the role of muse in my life's work
as caretaker of art, general of genius:
      borrowed glory.
Stieglitz mutters. Something, work is startling,
something, paint-poet, infantile visionary.

Like a piece of ice in the mouth, this moment,
this moment will not last.

On meeting, his eyes expressed disappointment
that he <u>could not</u> desire me.

The Jackal is below but the turning of the day can make him rise. Failure is always there, waiting. Sinuous enough to slip through any gap. Listen, you can hear the click, click of the wheel. Today it is mired in mud and the horse cannot pull the cart. Tomorrow, the spinning wheel turns unencumbered, and I do not prick my finger, not once. The flax turns to gold. That old tale, you have heard it, haven't you? When he stamps, he rips his own leg off in fury. All those golden winged things. Was it worth it? Pyrite, piles of it, each room is full of it. When I touch the golden rocks they crumble like old biscuits, circular pieces roll on and on, vanishing into the spaces in the floorboards. O. That is why we feel hunger; we cannot gather them to find the way out. When the orange beast walks around the rooms his claws tap on the floor like a piano player practicing scales. Yellow eyes stare from behind the hyacinth plant that rests on the looming instrument.

Green sheaf, but not a leaf,
dollars, thickly wadded.
Thirteen copies will be made,
Thirteen shillings for the year,
Thirteen pence a copy,
Thirteen lunar moons.
Judas was the thirteenth man.
All he ever wanted was to be
noticed, to be the first pair
of eyes sought out in the room.
Even as he betrayed Jesus
he only did it to be locked
with his Lord forever,
closer than a maggot
in a yellow plum.

A stunted tree with four
branches awash with leaves.
Fat, grasping hands –
they are sketched with thick
black ink on cream paper,
shaped like maple
or giant poison ivy.

A bird who sits
on the wrist
by choice
will always hunt
better.
O! Bring back more rabbits –
more than than one
who is kept tied to a post.

Landscape of white rocks. A door is locked, and the key is made of pale blancmange and will not hold together. It is daylight but an old man approaches, carrying a lamp. His grey robes hang as if damp. Sodden. I have forgotten to order new charcoal. The fire will not burn, despite blowing on the embers. No visitors! A small hut in a forest, with only the sound of badgers snuffling and wood pigeons *don't go, dancing, please don't go dancing, don't.* Shadow cave, with bats swooping, or an abandoned castle, with only one liveable room. The fridge-cold walls thick as a body – skulls and rust-brown swords rooted beneath the moat.

Ruth Stacey

I draw what is true, not
what is pretty. I am so petty
I conjure spells in the hope of turning
them porcine. I am a miniature Circe,
dressed in a brown shawl.
Nothing works, but I eat bacon
for lunch and chew them hard.
I drink too much in the evening
and owe my friends money.
I paint nine swords onto the wall
beside my bed. Each one cuts me.
I bath in ice cold water to punish
myself for the sin.

Despite searching pots and drawers, only five coins.
Not sovereigns. One shilling,
four pence.

A lighthouse is manned by a man without a name.
He goes quite mad and forgets
to light it.

Perhaps, someone will realise, or no great ships
will need to traverse those rocks
this evening.

Five small plates laid on the table to be filled.
One with dead roses. One with sawdust.
Three filled with black water.

There is an empty riverbed full of dying fish. The light continues to soak into the greyness and turn it to colour. I automatically list the shades in my mind, but the peach and lavender of dawn is otherworldly and refuses to give answers. The building opposite has a woman stencilled on the side selling soap. Clean and creamy. I think that she is Justice, her arms held out to embrace me. One hand holds success, the other failure. Her painted eyes are ugly and uneven.

Feel Everything!

To walk for miles along the streets until the internal compass realises the body is too far from home, and with a sigh, the flesh spins and returns in the same footsteps. A planet with two moons circling it. Far off, a smaller star, watching this celestial dance. Alone. Always at a hem, an ankle. Never inside the magic circle. Imagine an unpeelable orange. The flesh uneaten, whilst in another space apples shed their skins in one long curl, like sheer-silk stockings discarded on a chair. O! Burning unburnt Lady! O! Rosy cheeked one! O! White-blouse! Let me be your black waistcoat. Pick me! Speak into a cave, expect an echo, but there is silence. Plane tree leaves blow along the street. Cat slinks behind me, a tabby shadow. My glamour works for him alone.

Europe! A tower on fire,
the foundations ruined.

Lightning has struck us all.
We stare in astonishment,

babies mewing. How are
we still breathing air

in this inferno? Men
used as materials to build

something. Ossuary. We make
toys, craft small books to sell

for the fingertips that reach.
The great-weary city is full of

vehicles huffing out fumes.
Khaki lines, grey blankets.

In the sky, a red sun, with
the Queen of Heaven's face.

Flames of blue-white halo
flare towards the West.

The colours are gone. Everything is reduced to black lines and sepia. Each composer sounds different. I am trudging down the street to post a letter in my once purple robe. Nature unnerves me, with its constant changing of weather and seasons. I pull my felt hat over my ears against the bite of the morning. I prefer a stage, which can be dressed at will. Curtains open; from my seat it could be an ice kingdom or a forest. Props move, backdrops lift and fall. The ropes creak, weights rise, it is summer. Stagehands wind the winch, and it is winter. A man hangs suspended from the curtain ropes, but it is a trick of the light and I see that he is only there to drop snow onto Desdemona. In that moment, the artifice slips away, and it is real.

VIII

A Small Bown Book To Fit In A Pocket

O DEARY me how idle is
This great and weary town.
For people talk and never do
As they go up and down.
– **Pamela Colman Smith, The Green Sheaf, No.11, 1904.**

Pixie is as delightful as ever and has a big roomed flat near Victoria Station with black walls and orange curtains. She is now an ardent and pious Roman Catholic, which has added to her happiness but taken from her friends. She now has the dullest of friends, selected entirely because they are R.C. converts most of them, half-educated people, who want to see both eyes in a profile drawing. She goes to confession every Sunday – except the week I was there – she couldn't think of any sins, so my influence must have been very holy. – **Lily Yeats, J.B Yeats Letters, Ed. Hone, p.162.**

Darling Edy [...] Make Picky buck up and send me something by return to work on [...] Love from Your Baby.' – **Christopher St John (Chris) to Edy Craig, letter, (ET archive D2198).**

Blithe Pixie, singing Yeats' songs, or telling West Indian tales with her bright painted dolls. In later life she took to drink and embarrassed her friends over series of unpaid loans. – **John Masefield, Some Memories of W.B Yeats, 1940.**

Miss Coleman Smith, an old friend and penitent of mine is, as you know, buying a house at the Lizard and I believe undertaking the welfare of the mission there [...] she has been a staunch and faithful friend for many years. – **Monseigneur Henry O'Brien, Letter held by Plymouth Diocese, 1919.**

Miss Balfour managed to get an invalid priest who does all he can but Miss Smith has not been too pleased with his help or too considerate when he is not well enough. The whole position is rather irregular [...] – **Bishop of Plymouth, to Madame Roberts, Letter held by Plymouth Diocese, October 6th, 1927.**

If I could get sale from my work –and some capital to work with – all would be well but things seem to get worse instead of better. Do please think of something, suggest something. I write to you distracted, Corinne. Mrs Lake is sure you make a good suggestion. She is still in bed and sends greetings. – **Pamela Colman Smith, letter to Nellie, Letter held by Plymouth Diocese, 1927.**

I give devise and bequeath all my estate both real and personal to my friend Nora Lake. – **Pamela Colman Smith, Last Will and Testament, February 23rd, 1951.**

Chosen in haste, like many of the things Pamela did, this book was found to have mould-yellow paper inside and was not an aesthetic thing to write or draw in. Pamela had left her black and orange London flat and purchased a long-term lease on a house called Parc Garland in 1919, with a bequest from an American relative. Windswept, situated on the Lizard at the tip of the Cornish peninsula. There was a tiny chapel, which Pamela christened Our Lady of the Lizard, and the hope was to expand the Catholic faith amongst the resistant Cornish folk. She wrote many letters imploring for help to get her church started. Lacking not larking. Her housekeeper, Nora Lake, had a husband to do the garden, but he was so dull he turned into a tree one day and nobody noticed. Or perhaps he died in the second World War. The two women, and Mrs Lake's ineffectual son Freddie, left the chapel and moved to Bude. Freddie faded from the story. The women found themselves to be the most comfortable of companions, like two little mammals who made a nest for themselves. Despite illness, and mutual caring duties, they lived out their days together until Pamela's heart burst. This book was dropped into a well by a priest who visited Pamela, now calling herself Corinne, in the last of her cloud-wisp guises. She had pressed it into his hands and asked him to keep it safe. However, he read it that night, shivering, and the next day cast it into a well at the monastery, believing it to be blasphemous.

Passport photo 1916. Reproduced with kind permission from Pamela Colman Smith: The Untold Story US Games Inc. (2018)

Jesus comes to me in a dream.
Burrow dark, the room breathes in
the dust motes of dawn.
The mirror is a dull, leaden disc,
nailed above the hand-made
cedar dresser he gave as a gift.
Wine, red as a healing wound,
tastes like the inside of his mouth.
Behind him, the continent of his wife
breaches the black ocean of the bed.
Her breath raises the linen landscape,
disturbing the silence.
His face is nothing but dark absences
with the lighter cross of brow
and the blade-slash of the nose.
Approached, the mirror only shows one
quarter of a portrait at a time.
One eye pinned, one cheek studied.
Solemn from a distance, close up
the grin cuts the face like an axe
in the trunk of a tree.
There is an animal curve
to this smile; the charisma
of it can draw anyone to him –
it is a mage's spell.

Spring festival in a little village. Men carry rods decorated with flowers. A wreath forms a circle of leaves above us all. In every direction: fields. Put your back into it. Push, pull, plant. A hare speaks to a rainbow I paint, through a spider web I break. Church built on a rock is far away on the horizon; it turns from a small grey blur to a magnificent stone monolith. Skin is like paper. The clouds part and reveal a hand; it entreats to be held. Little sticks in the hearth, sparked, become a fire. The beads on the rosary are so comforting in their unending circle. The incense curls: black paint mixed with grey and swirled with a horsehair brush transfers it to an image. I write how fun it is to be Catholic.

Ave, Maris Stella!
Establish us in peace, meek and blessed.
The chapel is open night and day, the phrases
of the sea crash below, salt thick in the air,
gulls fly in circles far above us all.
The low sound of a voice at vespers
mixes with the wind and rain.
Pure in mind. Chaste in action.
Mother above all mothers, hear my prayer,
I am your devoted benefactress perched
on this rock at the end of all ends.
Ships full of men fought battles on the horizon.
I see their past lives in my dreams, Spanish
Armada, wooden forest of souls, or torpedoed wool
uniforms sinking down into the deep: to you.
Frail is our vessel, and the ocean is wide.
Steer the vessel of our lives to the quiet haven
of our heart's desire, star of the sea, mer-mother.

Daub paint roughly onto thick paper; waves deserve frantic creation. Imbue each sweep with the energy of the paintbrush. I see you, Lyonesse; I see you Lethowsow. There, just below the waves: turrets, church spires and gables reaching for the sky. Filled with salt-water, houses host seaweed and the fish shoals' pirouette through your streets. Where is God? they cried, as storms destroyed their beautiful churches built in his honour. With you. The sun continued to shine as He absorbed you into his depths. There is a time for everything. Seven rocks form a bridge between here and elsewhere. We smile as we overhear fisherman murmur in the dock about sailing close to the sea-city. Milk-white water rushes around the reefs. A day-trip to St Michael's Mount, the delicious fear of the tide trapping us on this island. Karrek Loos yn Koos, the grey rock in the woods. Now the woodland is below the sea; driftwood collected on leisurely afternoon walks is evidence of God's plan for tender transformation.

The secret tree is not a secret:
it stands on the edge of the field,
roots seeking water in the brook.

Old Man Willow, your nooks are rooms
for hedgehogs, your limbs shape the den
that is supposed to be secret.

Do not tell anyone, a child says.
All children fear me, yet I made stories
for children. I help him climb.

His shoe slips from his foot and falls
deep into the tree, his sister
breaks a stick and pokes the darkness,

retrieves it and silences all tears.
Children of my body unborn,
they do not live and cannot die.

Voices rustle in the wind-blown leaves.
Don't tell anyone this green tale:
the secret tree is now your secret.

Sand beneath the feet, toes gripping minuscule rocks ground to powder. Kneeling on the beach, about to rise, caught in a photograph. Remembering the holiday, the same beach. Caves gape open like blackened mouths. The cliff rock is grey and jagged. Dream shades of friends appear wrapped in turbans and blankets. There will be ham and hard-boiled eggs for lunch, salt twisted in paper for the tomatoes. Growing older is like a donkey carrying a saddle, then baskets, rolls of cloth, bags of grain. Each burden weighing the small back and hoofs down. Slight grimace at being snapped. Edy stands to one side, looking towards me. Chris stands between us, solidly wrapped in white. My pale legs unused to the sun; nape and shoulders curve like a daffodil past the moment to be harvested. The sabbath bells ring out, drifting dragonflies settle, there is an apple for each of us.

No weapon is needed in this place.
There are no barbs hidden, you only want
to teach me about the other world,
to show me the lion that lives inside myself.
Honey makes it behave. I feed it.
There is a door in everyone.
Here is the key, given without judgement.
Go back in time when robes were
long and sleeves rang with bells.
Monks carry prayer books
in cloisters, the windows open
to the elements.
I can go there anytime and my beast
will let me stroke his face.
Teeth graze my skin but do not bite.

It is the hill by the cliff. One wrist flick and it is created on the page. The hill is stoic. A dog sits on the cliff and the wind is fierce; it is a mammal with warm blood, and it is unflinching. The wind whips its long ears and still it faces the storm. Hill is earth piled high; it creates ballast against the incoming weather. Perhaps the dog is made of the hill. Mud-dog, crawl back to your master. The wind used to be blood-warm and the grass swayed; now it is whipped. It was always sunny, now it seems endlessly grey. The grass is flinching, I watch it falter and wave. Green is actually many kinds of brown and tan and yellow, you learn this when you paint it. Colour is just warmth that catches the trembling eye. The thunder comes now. Nora helps me to the window so I can watch. Storms are electric strings that cringe when they touch our earth. It strikes the hill. I wave at the grass as it flinches beneath the rain.

Asleep on the settee
in the afternoon sun, my sketchbook
fallen to the floor and Nora's knitting
gathered in her lap like a blue kitten,
I wake from a dream where I
got paid for my artwork and we ate
steak and caviar for dinner.
Instead, we will have toast and thin jam.
This room is a globe. I papered
it with my drawings. Listen.
Nora's snores are primal, cave-deep,
my large, growly bear.
I admire the white hair
that curls around the seashell of her ear.
I allow myself to idly wallow in this
half- sleep of waking. Each memory
a pleasant pale-yellow sin to confess.
Nora opens her hazel eyes
and calls me her mole.

Bencoolen House named after a shipwreck, contains wrecked ships. Bodies are nothing but fully rigged ships for the soul. Old age dashes, bashes, hurls the body onto rocks. Nora cannot send out a distress rocket for this danger; it lies unlit. Cannot walk, cannot draw. Can. Not. Candle. Nothing. Only the movement of the sea sounds animated. Pulled by one ball of rock. My head turns to follow the waxing and waning. I resemble a whole, half, crescent into blackness. White marble statues were painted, did you know? Garish colours removed for purity, aspiration. Humans are imperfect though. Place blue against red, reflect the vein and what it contains. Rub the skin to try and make the slow blood show.

Plough, hang low in the firmament, moon high.
Long nights rot the plant life away, unhindered.
Branches twine like clasped fingers,
bones against the grey, brown, grey of soil-sky.
Frost suck the honey from my comb.
Lean against bark and be indistinguishable,
deplete my covetous flesh to little sticks.
Air moist with unspent rain, turn bitter now.
Fall and cover her skin like dust sheets.
Obliterate all sounds and smells; shush.
The casement windows are stuck.
Peel an apple, slowly. The longing is for life,
but quietly. I want to let the frozen air in.
Do not leave the key beneath the mat – stay!
Songbirds like cotton reels, peck the bottles of milk
for the cream. Cat wants to unravel one.

Dragon and Knight overlook the pews. Animals dance against clouds. Drag a thread through the unceasing muddle of the maze. A skein of wool to lead me out. Someone has hand-coloured it and it is a smudge of ash, or heather, or mud. Suggestion of a colour. The sparrows ate the breadcrumbs: let them, it wasn't cake, it was brioche. Maze, confuse, lead astray. Disguises are for sale in that shop on the corner. Shall we try them on for fun? You can be the French Queen and I will be a courtier in yellow banded stockings. Always touch the left side and you will get out. New hedges are planted, the herbs are not tall enough, yew saplings have grown to close the gaps where we could escape. If the cattle break the fence they will die if they eat the berries. Put it in the churchyard. My darling, all the unwritten pages in the diary were happy days. Can you find your way through the headstones? There is a little door, the lintel is curved sandstone and the pauper's graves are unmarked.

Echo, who hides behind the sheltering hills,
Sad Echo – always shy,
Sometimes she will not come at all,
At others, always nigh.

PCS, Volume VII, The Green Sheaf

Pamela Colman Smith by Alice Boughton. The Literary Digest, July 4, 1908.

IX

Notes

Notes

This is a work of montage. Seven imagined memoirs introduced by primary sources, both from Pamela herself and her reviewers or friends, in the section before each memoir. Playful invented sources for my imaginary memoirs, and symbolist poems that create a first-person voice for Pamela Colman Smith to tell her story. Many of the poems contain direct inspiration from Pamela Colman Smith's pictures, letters and essays, including fragments and paraphrased words, and descriptions of images. This comes from my own archive research and the excellent research by Smith scholars: Elizabeth Foley O'Connor, Stuart R Kaplan, Melinda Boyd Parsons, Mary K Greer, Kathleen Pyne, Katherine Cockin, and Dawn G Robinson.

Letter Archives:

Pamela Colman Smith letters, 1896-1900. Archives of American Art, Smithsonian Institution

Pamela Colman Smith collection, Special Collections Department, Bryn Mawr College Library.

Alfred Stieglitz/Georgia O'Keeffe Archive, Yale Collection of American Literature. Beinecke Rare Book and Manuscript Library.

Ellen Terry and Edith Craig database. The papers are available for consultation for researchers by appointment, either at Smallhythe Place or the British Library.

Quoted Lines:

p.36 from *Annancy Tales* by Pamela Colman Smith, published by PH Russell, 1899

p.63 from Pamela Colman Smith Visitor Book, Stuart R Kaplan library

p.94 from *A Season in Hell* by Rimbaud

p.95 from a letter by PCS to Alfred Stieglitz, November 19, 1909

p.99 from 'Au Lecteur' by Baudelaire

Poem Acknowledgments:

'Colour is Distracting' published online by *Ink, Sweat and Tears* 2023.

'Asleep I can hear the spider' published by *Alcatraz: anthology of short prose and prose poetry*, Gazebo Books, Sydney 2023.

'Reveries, the wall is green' and 'Over the rim of the cup' published by *Contemporary Surrealist and Magical Realist Poetry, An International Anthology*, Lamar University Literary Press, 2022.

'It is the hill by the cliff' published by Abridged 0-82 'Axis, 2022.

'Pan, stars are banished' and 'Claude Debussy wants to tell me something' were published online by *and other poems* 2021.

Thank you to my supportive publisher Alec Newman who believes in my work and produces beautiful books, and Lawrence Stacey for designing my book cover.

I would like to thank Elizabeth Foley O'Connor for her support and generous friendship. I needed someone who also loved PCS. The *unsent poem to a cousin* is dedicated to you.

Gratitude to my supervisors, Tony Williams, and Katherine Baxter, without whom, I could not have achieved this piece of work.

Thank you to Luke Kennard and Jo Clement for their feedback on my work. It meant so much to me.

Thank you to Susanna and Stevie Ronnie for being excellent friends during my studies and giving me a place to stay.

Thank you to Cassandra Atherton who encouraged me and made me believe I could write prose poetry.

Thanks to Paul Hardwick, and Lucy Arnold, who gave me generous advice on the prose poetry chapter in my thesis; Amali Gunasekera, who I admire as a fellow contemporary symbolist; and to all other academics I have spoken to about the project and received encouragement from … thank you so much!

Thank you to Fiona Sampson and Carolyn Jess-Cooke for wise words at critical times, and friendship – at all times!

Thank you to my fellow Worcester academics in the School of Humanities, who have supported and encouraged me, especially Jack McGowan (I could not have finished this without your support and belief in me).

Thank you to my dear family and friends, for being patient and never telling me I should do something more down to earth than poetry.

www.ingramcontent.com/pod-product-compliance
Lightning Source LLC
Chambersburg PA
CBHW050816090426
42736CB00022B/3475